## Dreaming Verse

Edited By Lynsey Evans

First published in Great Britain in 2024 by:

Young Writers
Remus House
Coltsfoot Drive
Peterborough
PE2 9BF
Telephone: 01733 890066
Website: www.youngwriters.co.uk

All Rights Reserved
Book Design by Ashley Janson
© Copyright Contributors 2024
Softback ISBN 978-1-83565-418-7
Printed and bound in the UK by BookPrintingUK
Website: www.bookprintinguk.com
YB0590A

# FOREWORD

Welcome Reader, to a world of dreams.

For Young Writers' latest competition, we asked our writers to dig deep into their imagination and create a poem that paints a picture of what they dream of, whether it's a make-believe world full of wonder or their aspirations for the future.

The result is this collection of fantastic poetic verse that covers a whole host of different topics. Let your mind fly away with the fairies to explore the sweet joy of candy lands, join in with a game of fantasy football, or you may even catch a glimpse of a unicorn or another mythical creature. Beware though, because even dreamland has dark corners, so you may turn a page and walk into a nightmare!

Whereas the majority of our writers chose to stick to a free verse style, others gave themselves the challenge of other techniques such as acrostics and rhyming couplets.

Each piece in this collection shows the writers' dedication and imagination – we truly believe that seeing their work in print gives them a well-deserved boost of pride, and inspires them to keep writing, so we hope to see more of their work in the future!

# CONTENTS

## Batley Parish CE (VA) Junior, Infant & Nursery School, Batley

| | |
|---|---|
| Olivia Buckley (10) | 1 |
| Maryam Sophia Qadri (10) | 2 |
| Keyaan Salloo (10) | 4 |
| Alisha Kiani (10) | 6 |

## Brynteg CP School, Brynteg

| | |
|---|---|
| Oliver Jones (10) | 7 |
| Callum Adams (11) | 8 |
| Annie Marubbi (10) | 10 |
| Dexter Tudor (10) | 11 |
| Ashton Saleh (11) | 12 |
| Imogen Grace Tudor (10) | 13 |
| Frankee Davies (10) | 14 |
| Carys Green (11) | 15 |
| David Lovin (10) & Chloe Sandra Adams (9) | 16 |
| Madison Elson (10) | 17 |
| Eira Blake (11) | 18 |
| Finley Brimfield (11) | 19 |
| Cameron Jones (10) | 20 |
| Kyson James Davies (9) | 21 |
| Tom Jones (10) | 22 |
| Josh Woodward (11) | 23 |
| George Stone (10) | 24 |
| Zayan Uddin (9) | 25 |

## Galston Primary School, Galston

| | |
|---|---|
| Robbie Campbell (9) | 26 |
| Quinn Hamilton (9) | 28 |
| Lilley-Rose Murray (9) | 30 |
| Vhairi Griffiths (9) | 31 |
| Luca Newall (9) | 32 |

| | |
|---|---|
| Isaac King (9) | 33 |
| Gracie Stevenson (9) | 34 |
| Aaran Boore (9) | 35 |
| Ava Elder (9) | 36 |
| Haniya Munir (9) | 37 |
| Mitchell Clark (9) | 38 |
| Falyn Adams (9) | 39 |
| Katie Skilling (10) | 40 |
| Ellis Williamson (9) | 41 |
| Joey McFarlane (9) | 42 |
| John Stebbings (9) | 43 |
| Jamie Downie (9) | 44 |
| Niamh Murray (9) | 45 |
| Effie McCutcheon (9) | 46 |
| Ellie-Máe Haining (9) | 47 |
| Kian Anderson (9) | 48 |

## Malvern Primary School, Belfast

| | |
|---|---|
| Indie-Skye Adams (10) | 49 |
| Antony Joby (11) | 50 |
| Lily Green (10) | 52 |
| Eve Harris (10) | 53 |
| Ethan Huston (10) | 54 |
| Maisie Butler (9) | 55 |
| Riley Gray (11) | 56 |
| Lukas Darragh Stewart (9) | 57 |
| Ethan O'Hara (11) | 58 |
| Jacob Scott (10) | 59 |

## Mobile Play In Action, Airdrie

| | |
|---|---|
| Alicja McLean (10) | 60 |
| Holly Moffat (11) | 61 |
| Keeva Cowan (9) | 62 |
| Chloe Longridge (10) | 63 |

| | |
|---|---|
| Max Murray (9) | 64 |
| Emmy Armitage (9) | 65 |
| Stephanie Stewart (10) | 66 |
| Gavin Roberts (10) | 67 |
| Thea Roscoe (9) | 68 |

## Newbridge-On-Wye Church in Wales School, Newbridge-On-Wye

| | |
|---|---|
| Bella Beehan (9) | 69 |
| Jameela Cameela Akyaw (9) | 70 |
| Luna Kezze (8) | 71 |
| Caitlyn Watling (7) | 72 |
| Freya Hobbs (8) | 73 |
| Freyja Hounsome (8) | 74 |
| Evie Millard (9) | 75 |
| Efa Allison (8) | 76 |
| Ralph Smith (7) | 77 |
| Teddy Smith (8) | 78 |
| Max Prosser (8) | 79 |
| Caiden Thomas (7) | 80 |
| Archie Cullum (8) | 81 |
| Finn Samuel (8) | 82 |
| Regan Christie-Rees (8) | 83 |
| Lily Waters (8) | 84 |
| Oliver Jones (9) | 85 |
| John Meredith (8) | 86 |
| Paige Baynham (7) | 87 |
| William Savage Samuel (8) | 88 |
| Aneurin Edwards (7) | 89 |

## Our Lady Of Victories RC Primary School, London

| | |
|---|---|
| Victoire Deconinck (8) | 90 |
| Romy Treguer (8) | 91 |

## Our Lady Queen Of Peace Catholic Primary School, Litherland

| | |
|---|---|
| Amelia Henners (10) | 92 |
| Michelle Etuk (10) | 93 |

| | |
|---|---|
| Millie Hannan (9) | 94 |
| Elisha Odeh (10) | 95 |
| Pippa King (10) | 96 |
| Sophie Dears (9) | 97 |
| Ava Devlin (9) | 98 |
| Evie Hughes (10) | 99 |

## Rice Lane Primary School, Liverpool

| | |
|---|---|
| Lottie Cole (11) | 100 |
| Harriet Coady-Taylor (9) | 102 |
| Sofia Tyrrell (10) | 103 |
| Phoebe Edwards (10) | 104 |
| Paul Atkinson (10) | 105 |
| Mya-Rose Rice (11) | 106 |
| Myla Woodward (8) & Isla | 107 |
| M Patrick (10) | 108 |
| Cali Gray (9) & Connie Corker (9) | 109 |
| Sophie Cunliffe (9) & Emily McDermott (8) | 110 |
| Olivia Wood (10) | 111 |
| Darcy Teer (9) | 112 |
| Poppy Hart (8) | 113 |
| Quinn Pruden (10) | 114 |
| Marley Dainton King (9) | 115 |

## St Andrew's CE Junior School, Burnham-On-Sea

| | |
|---|---|
| Maria Sobin (9) | 116 |
| Laicey Fowler (9) | 117 |
| Maddison Davies (7) | 118 |
| Freya Jeffries (9) | 119 |
| Morgana Cameron (9) | 120 |
| Sofia Hall (8) | 121 |
| Fynnley Strange (9) | 122 |
| Frankie Pini (7) | 123 |
| Mabel-Rose Warrilow (9) | 124 |

## St Joseph's RC Primary School, Hurst Green

| | |
|---|---|
| Charlie Maudsley (10) | 125 |
| Joe Canty (9) | 126 |
| Emma McCrea (11) | 128 |
| Penny Grace Rowland (10) | 130 |
| Sarah McCrea (11) | 131 |
| Samuel Wilkinson (11) | 132 |
| Celia Milligan (10) | 133 |
| Harrison Holden (9) | 134 |
| Athealia Sumner (11) | 136 |
| Fatima Alshahada (10) | 137 |
| Daisy Moorby (10) | 138 |
| Lucy Wilkinson (9) | 139 |
| Florence Meadows (10) | 140 |
| Zach Falencki (9) | 141 |
| Bracken James (10) | 142 |
| William Dilworth (9) | 143 |
| Tom McNeela (10) | 144 |
| Grace Elizabeth Hardman (9) | 145 |
| Sebastian (9) | 146 |
| Ellie Grix (9) | 147 |
| Freddy Jackson (10) | 148 |
| Alexander Backshall (10) | 149 |
| Gus Morley (11) | 150 |

## St Martin's School, Bournemouth

| | |
|---|---|
| Evie Champion (10) | 151 |
| Martha Callear (10) | 152 |
| Lucy Auger (9) | 153 |
| Connie Watts (9) | 154 |
| Freddie Mussell (9) | 155 |
| Maya Benstead-Brooks-Dravecz (9) | 156 |
| Rufus Stevens (9) | 157 |
| Alex Broit (9) | 158 |
| Rory Dennis (9) | 159 |
| Teddy Barker-Stock (9) | 160 |
| Finn Dennis (9) | 161 |
| Rupert Spencer (9) | 162 |

## Winwick CE Primary School, Winwick

| | |
|---|---|
| Alice Walker (7) | 163 |
| Alyssa Riley (7) | 164 |
| Sophia Reeves (7) | 165 |
| Asianne Chaudhry (8) | 166 |
| George Lever (7) | 167 |
| Esme Tilley-Stoneman (7) | 168 |
| Arjun Kankonkar (7) | 169 |
| Charlie Cookson (7) | 170 |
| Ella Anders (7) | 171 |
| Olive Morris (7) | 172 |
| Jake Thomas (7) | 173 |
| James Bower (7) | 174 |
| Isaac Cotterill (7) | 175 |
| Jack Holligan (8) | 176 |

# THE POEMS

# The Endless Dream

Once I had this dream,
It was so real,
I couldn't compare it to reality,
I stood in my room, quiet, no sound,
My jaw dropped to see a little void, just standing around,
As it got bigger my nerves got quicker,
I fell into this void,
I felt my life destroyed,
After endless minutes I stood before a door,
Three, no more,
I chose the middle door,
The first one I saw was a weird land standing before my feet,
I leapt inside,
All of a sudden a man was staring at me,
He offered his hand with a glee,
I took it but I vanished into this fantasy cloud as I fell from the sky,
I saw my worst nightmare,
A clown stood before my eyes,
Before I could speak, I woke up back to reality.

**Olivia Buckley (10)**
Batley Parish CE (VA) Junior, Infant & Nursery School, Batley

# Echo

I walk down the hallway,
The smell of woody perfume intrudes,
Blue and green shadows dance through the doorway,
I transcend into the living room.

The blue and green lights are swirling,
Swirling round a circular device,
The swirling becomes murmuring,
It's not so silent and not so nice.

There's swirling and a voice,
My heart jumps in my chest,
The voice is a familiar noise,
This is turning into a dangerous quest.

"How may I help you?" she says,
A voice, perfectly calm and measured,
"Ask me, what can I do for you?" she threatens.
A voice, robotic, that has me pressured.

Swirling lights and the voice threatening,
I run as fast as I can,
It has me twirling, and my face sweating,
The voice I know all too well.

Suddenly, I wake up,
It was a dream, *phew!*
I still have my luck!
"How may I help you?"
I hear her spew!

## Maryam Sophia Qadri (10)
Batley Parish CE (VA) Junior, Infant & Nursery School, Batley

# The Nightmare Of Freddy's

I awaken from bed,
A sound from the closet,
Is what I dread,
All that gossip,
Echoes through the halls,
I hear footsteps,
It falls,
In the depths.

Freddy with a top hat,
He's not a teddy bear,
I can't tap,
He loves to scare.

Chica with a cupcake,
She has a large beak,
Oh for goodness sake,
She likes to make me shriek.

Bonnie Bonnie with bunny ears,
He wears a red bowtie,
He always peers,
It makes me want to cry.

Foxy, he has a mighty hook,
He also has a long tongue,
He gives me a grimace look,
Something is wrong.

I am scared,
Where can I hide?
I feel all teary-eyed,
They come in with pride.

**Keyaan Salloo (10)**
Batley Parish CE (VA) Junior, Infant & Nursery School, Batley

# My Dream

I opened my eyes only to find out I was in a dream,
I've always wanted a friendship team,
And it happened in the middle of March; the unluckiest month for me,
Someone was talking to me but it was a bee.
I saw someone selling ice cream so big,
They were also wearing an ice cream wig.
When I reached for ice cream, I was in bed,
Next to me was a note saying my sister hadn't been fed.
So that was my dream,
I still hope I can get a friendship team!

**Alisha Kiani (10)**
Batley Parish CE (VA) Junior, Infant & Nursery School, Batley

# Liverpool Is Coming For Glory

In my dreams every night,
I had a dream about Liverpool FC Football Club.
Suddenly I woke up somewhere I had never been before!
I was excited but scared.
I looked to my side and saw the manager, Klopp.
I was so excited to see what he said to me!
"Well, we have heard a lot about you, Oliver Jones," he said.
"What is it?"
"You are good enough to play for your dream team, Liverpool," he said.
"Yes!" I jumped in excitement.
It was my debut 90+6 minutes
Against Man United in the final,
To win the treble there was one minute left,
It was a free-kick to us and I was taking the free-kick.
I went to hit the ball, it went sideways, it was all up to me, I shot!
Suddenly the ball started to curl into the top bins,
*Bang!* It hit the net,
Yes, yes, to make it 2-3 to us!

**Oliver Jones (10)**
Brynteg CP School, Brynteg

# The Nightmare

This is a nightmare
The animatronics are trying to get into my room.

Is that Freddy?
He looks like a teddy
The clock ticks
Why can't it just be six?
This has to be a nightmare.

Come on, the second day
They must repay
I go from door to door
How can these wooden doors protect me from animatronic monsters?

The third day comes
The fox is in my closet
He scares me
Who's on my bed?
Oh it's Freddy
*This has to be a nightmare.*

Come on, two days till the party
But you still come and get me
Come on Foxy
I have to fight to see the bright.

Is that Fredbear?
Come on, it's only him
This has to be a nightmare
If I fight I'll see the bright.

**Callum Adams (11)**
Brynteg CP School, Brynteg

# Candyland

I was fast asleep in my bed, dreaming about a land.
Where everywhere you looked you saw sweets.
Either having a chat or washing their strawberry lace hair.
I could see marshmallows going down a slide into a pool full of chocolate,
I took another look around and said to myself, "Wow, this is so cool!"
I started running around until I got stopped by a giant doughnut.
He took me to a museum where I saw a dragon and his chocolate wings.
At the end of our tour, he told me his name,
It was Ben, after that, I left at ten.

**Annie Marubbi (10)**
Brynteg CP School, Brynteg

# The Mine

I'm stuck somewhere random, far away.
Am I in the night or the day?
All I see is a cart, an old one.
I hear a rumble behind me.
And now I'm scared!
It rumbles and rattles
And races down the path.
I better go fast!
I'm in a... I'm in a... I'm in a mine
And I ain't feeling fine!

I come across a bridge,
With my rolling vehicle.
It's old and broken. Watch out!
Rocking and rolling,
Can I make it over?
And yes I do!
Then I see a bright light
And I get out!

**Dexter Tudor (10)**
Brynteg CP School, Brynteg

# The Promotion Dream

When I sleep at night,
Some dreams give me a fright,
The dream I could see,
Was a stadium and a tree,
The floodlight shone so bright,
The sight was nice, but could it be?
Ryan Reynolds and Rob McElhenney!
Less than a mile from the centre of the town,
People in Deadpool costumes walk up and down,
Now I'm signed for Wrexham,
Premier League is the dream,
But now I'm feeling a lot of fatigue,
We got a promotion, that was what we need,
I am living my dream.

**Ashton Saleh (11)**
Brynteg CP School, Brynteg

# Cats And Hats

There were cats,
And cats wearing smelly old hats,
I was so so happy,
Ah, so so yappy.
I took them all home,
And they met my garden gnome,
I cleaned them all up,
And they had a drink out of my cup.
I bought a cotton candy house,
But in the walls I found a mouse,
I had to get rid of it quick!
So I phoned a man and he gave it a kick,
But he ate everything,
And we never saw the mouse again,
But lucky enough we bought a house,
On Candy Cane Lane!

**Imogen Grace Tudor (10)**
Brynteg CP School, Brynteg

# Mystery Mushroom

In my dreams,
I could see a beautiful girl next to me,
She smelt like petals,
Her name was Pettale,
Her friends called her Ceri,
But she was smelly,
On the walk what we saw frightened me!
It was a mushroom, but not a normal mushroom,
It was a big green mushroom with purple spots like lavender,
We knocked on the door but it was locked,
But what happened next was a shock,
The door opened after we went in,
But the potion they took was in a mystery book.

**Frankee Davies (10)**
Brynteg CP School, Brynteg

# The Mysterious House

One mysterious time, I see lots of
Sweets on this house, but there is no
One in the house. There is a portal
And, when I go through, it is a desert.
I have a football with me, and there
Is a really, really tall man. I
Call him Jack. So I throw the
Football at his head, and he falls
To the floor. I wake in this
Mysterious house and someone
Comes out of the house, and
I try to run out, but the portal has
Closed. I am in danger, and I
Am trapped.

**Carys Green (11)**
Brynteg CP School, Brynteg

# The Horror Night

I woke up at night,
I had a massive fright,
I looked under my bed,
I saw a dead head,
I screamed my guts out,
Then my mum said, "What was that about?"
"There's a dead head under my bed!"
My mum said, "Don't be scared, it's only your stepmum,
There's nothing to say,
Don't make a fuss,
She was kicking our minibus,
Don't make a hoot,
Now go find her missing boot!"

**David Lovin (10) & Chloe Sandra Adams (9)**
Brynteg CP School, Brynteg

# The Fright Maze

I am trapped here, it is truly a nightmare,
But I still cannot bear.
The trees are snowy,
And the bushes are glowy.
I see a maze,
Stuck with all these trees it puts me in a daze.
The moon shines so bright,
It makes everything a fright.
The dragons soar through the air,
Spreading their wings with flair.
I have such a nerve,
The path starts to curve.
Am I getting out of here,
To escape this fear?

**Madison Elson (10)**
Brynteg CP School, Brynteg

# The Forgiven World

I can see love and power beyond desire,
But with each cast comes a deadly fire.
If you love your family,
You better keep toe to toe,
Otherwise, your family will be taken alive.
You better hope they survive.
Your mistake, your family will never catch a break.
Stay at home during the night,
Then in the morning there will be no fight.
A deadly mistake is yours to make,
So this is where it ends, it depends.

**Eira Blake (11)**
Brynteg CP School, Brynteg

# The Mysterious Island

I am Jack Sparrow,
I can see trees on the horizon,
Me and my dog Gizmo,
Are searching for the mysterious island,
I am worried, scared, stunned, fascinated,
I have reached the island,
It is just amazing,
I will go to bed,
But I spot a bright light,
In the rocky mountain,
I decide that we will go,
To claim the light,
Tomorrow we start the hunt.

**Finley Brimfield (11)**
Brynteg CP School, Brynteg

# The Forest

I could see loads of trees around me,
I felt nervous, depressed and worried,
We were in the forest and woods,
We got caught, but we got away,
There was a dead end, and we had to hide in a bush,
Then we carried on running as fast as we could.

**Cameron Jones (10)**
Brynteg CP School, Brynteg

# Fortnite Dream

Heals and shields,
Pain and train,
Fortnite is such a great game,
But my mum says it will rot my brain!

I really don't care,
Because nothing was ever there,
Just an empty skull,
Covered in brown hair.

**Kyson James Davies (9)**
Brynteg CP School, Brynteg

# My Job Dream

Marine biology is dead
And dark to see.
You can go to the seabed,
But there is a fee.
He touched the seabed with a hurt knee.
He waved to the fish with a happy smile.
But he needed a wee.
He swam to the surface.

**Tom Jones (10)**
Brynteg CP School, Brynteg

# The House

I was in the woods,
Scared by myself,
Then I saw a house in sight,
Without a thought,
I ran off in a flash,
But then I fell over,
And got a rash,
I got up and saw,
The tree looked like a house.

**Josh Woodward (11)**
Brynteg CP School, Brynteg

# My Dream Job

Piloting is dangerous,
But I don't care,
Up in the sky is where I want to be,
With a posh uniform and dapper hair,
Pilots are great, it's clear to see,
And it will always be.

**George Stone (10)**
Brynteg CP School, Brynteg

# The Gingerbread Man

The gingerbread man looked so funny,
I bet he tastes oh, so, yummy!
Running through my dream,
I know he will scream
Once I catch him!
And I eat him and
Wake up from my dream!

**Zayan Uddin (9)**
Brynteg CP School, Brynteg

# I Want To Go Back

I walked into an eerie nostalgic room that felt confined,
A sofa as grey as silver and a blanket as dull red as a dead apple,
*I want to leave.*

It was like a room you couldn't escape,
An uncomfortable feeling,
A bright light above the room flashing as a light beam,
Plain colours as plain as a blank wall filled the room,
*I want to leave.*

The suspicious feel the room gave off as if I wasn't meant to be there,
It wasn't creepy but it was still and eerie,
I still couldn't tell if there was someone sitting on the couch,
*I want to leave.*

A small TV, I wondered if it worked,
Although the dream was short it had a deep meaning,
What is this small room? I want to know,
*I want to go back.*

A strange dream can question others like me,
You surely will see this dream has deflated me,
Will I ever escape my thoughts?
*I want to leave, I want to leave.*

**Robbie Campbell (9)**
Galston Primary School, Galston

# The White Maze

The long day finally ends.
I hop into my bed.
I'm not prepared for this nightmare,
Walls getting tighter and tighter the more I travel.
I hope it's over soon.

Tiny crawl spaces in the walls,
I don't understand why.
The time passes by.
I travel through the corners,
Hearing footsteps from the darkness,
As it breaks the silence.
Steps get louder and louder,
The closer they get.
I hope it's over soon.

I run back to the last crawl space I saw and hide in it.
I poke my head out and look.
A tall, black figure comes out,
Leaving bright, dark footprints, and leaves.
I hope it's over soon.

I leave and find a flashlight in the corner.
I rush to grab it.
The flashlight alerts the figure,
So I run into the darkness.
I find an exit and enter.
After that, I wake up.
I'm happy it is over.

**Quinn Hamilton (9)**
Galston Primary School, Galston

# The Magical Land

O nce I was writing a story about a magical land,
N early finished writing my story but somehow I fell in,
C learly, I was in my book, writing about a shadowy land which was frightening
E nchanting creatures in the sky.

U nicorns and pegasuses, even phoenixes,
P ink, purple and blue sparkles in the air like fireworks across the night sky,
O ver the moon, unicorns flew and pegasuses too,
N eon flowers dancing in the wind.

A round the corner I saw a forest, I saw the tallest tree ever.

D uring the walk through the forest, I met a tree that sneezed on me,
R unning around I was trying to catch a glowing firefly,
E very plant in the forest was magical,
A mountain was crying into a lake,
M uch unexpectedly I woke up in my bed.

**Lilley-Rose Murray (9)**
Galston Primary School, Galston

# The Magical Land Of Dreams

I open my eyes to a world full of surprise,
The world is dark and gloomy.
Smoke is everywhere,
Then I hear a dreadful sound,
The sound of an ancient clown,
Its giggles can be heard from all around.
Suddenly in a carnival on a tightrope, the clown starts to run,
The tightrope sways and I fall into the unknown,
I open my eyes to a world of surprise,
The world is as bright as the sun,
Mythical creatures dance about,
A unicorn says, "Oh please, come,"
Then we dance in the sun.
Magically, I climb on board,
He takes me high in the sky,
As we fly high in the sky I see the view through and through,
The bank is shocking pink,
The shops are sunlight-yellow,
We land in a gorgeous carnival with fairies everywhere,
Hours later I wake up with a grin on my face.

**Vhairi Griffiths (9)**
Galston Primary School, Galston

# The Forest Adventure

I was stranded in this abandoned forest,
Suddenly, I heard the wind sneezing constantly,
Every noise I hear, I fear,
Loudly, the storm roared,
Just at that moment, I heard a strange noise,
In the back, I wondered what had happened.

Just then, a squirrel jumped right in front of me,
I was scared and the ground rumbled,
The grass waved side to side,
I was running like Usain Bolt,
The storm rumbled like it was angry.

Then, I was exploring like a detective on a mission,
Suddenly, fog blew in like smoke,
But it went away quickly,
So I think it was a joke,
Strangely, I woke up to see I was safe in bed.

**Luca Newall (9)**
Galston Primary School, Galston

# Football

**F** un football is as fun as anything can be.
**O** verexcited to play at Hampden, like an adventurer exploring a new place.
**O** verjoyed after playing a football match, like a kid going on holiday.
**T** ime flies by at the match, as fast as Usain Bolt sprinting the 100m.
**B** rilliant game, the whistle blows for half-time, exhausted as a person running across the Sahara Desert.
**A** ll the fans cheered as loud as thunder.
**L** oving football, as adoring as a mum seeing her newborn baby for the first time.
**L** astly, the whistle blew, it was full-time I'm now as sad as a professional losing a game.

**Isaac King (9)**
Galston Primary School, Galston

# The Octopus

One by one, each of the girls looked about.
"Where are we?"
"I have no idea."
We started looking around.

Something octopus-like.
One tentacle came out like a slug,
Leaving slime all over the grass like a snake.

Then, one by one,
They kept popping out of each of the holes,
Like a meerkat scaring us.

Another tentacle came out,
Then another,
And took me into one of the holes!
*Swoosh!*

Down there, it was dark and scary.
All I heard was dripping from sharp, pointy rocks.
I didn't know that a giant octopus lived there...

**Gracie Stevenson (9)**
Galston Primary School, Galston

# My Acting Career

I went to bed,
Tired as a sloth,
I tucked myself in,
Not thinking about my dream.

I could see myself excited,
Sitting in a giant waiting room with white walls like snow,
An interviewer was waiting for me, her hair was like spider silk,
I was hired out of nowhere.

I could see myself joyful,
As I was practising my confusing script,
Was I really in a movie?
If the script could talk, it would say, 'You did it!'

I could see myself ecstatic as I was,
Making a movie with all my co-stars,
My acting skills were on point like a teacher's tick.

**Aaran Boore (9)**
Galston Primary School, Galston

# When I Could Fly

When I could fly,
I would smell the lovely minty air gently brushing off my face.

When I could fly,
I would taste the clouds,
To answer the question I had when I was young, "Does it taste like cotton candy?"

When I could fly,
I would touch the clouds, flying down on them as I stopped to rest in the sky.

When I could fly,
I would see the stars in the sky as they glimmered so brightly like diamonds.

When I could fly,
I would feel at peace because I was alone in the sky where no one could hurt me,
And as I slowly fell asleep I would be satisfied.

**Ava Elder (9)**
Galston Primary School, Galston

# The Castle

It is amazing,
I wake up in a giant castle in New York,
I don't have any work,
It's time to explore the city.
It will be a very fantastic day, be the perfect person to say it is wonderful.

I see the beautiful king and queen wearing shimmering clothes,
Sparkling like sequences, and
I am the princess, wearing a beautiful big ball gown,
An enormous gold round necklace,
And I am wearing a pretty gold crown on my head.

Suddenly, I wasn't in a giant castle,
Not even a battle,
Maybe some day I'll be there,
But not today!

**Haniya Munir (9)**
Galston Primary School, Galston

# The Vets

Finally, my dream came true.
Standing nervously, staring at the beautiful wounded dog,
Sad eyes looked up at me like waterfalls.
It was time for me to save him.
Eventually, I finished, it was so exciting, I saved him!
I was happy for myself and the dog.

Finally, my dreams came true.
I was scared of this because it looked hard.
It had a broken leg, so I had to concentrate.
The cast I put on it was one that had a picture of the cat.
Nervously, I waited for the cat to wake up.
After that I knew I wanted to be a vet.

**Mitchell Clark (9)**
Galston Primary School, Galston

# I Once Had A Dream

I once had a dream,
I was playing football at a stadium with my friends,
I could see lots of people watching me,
Only me,
I was creepy as a clown.

I felt cold and nervous,
Sometimes dreams cannot be nice,
They look really real,
It was the end of the game,
I went home,
Something was following me!

It was a fan,
They wanted me to write their autograph on their football,
I was running out of time,
I needed sleep,
But I quickly signed it,
I was finally famous!

**Falyn Adams (9)**
Galston Primary School, Galston

# When I Fell Asleep

When I fell asleep, I entered a magical world
I saw a fairy with bright pink wings
And a silky white dress making a popping potion

When I fell asleep, I entered a magical world
With a sunset sky, magic flew across the air
The grass turned from pink to blue
I thought I was delusional
Like a person who was hypnotised

When I fell asleep, I entered a magical world
The fairy gave me wings, a bedazzling dress
French plaits in my hair
And face gems like diamonds.

**Katie Skilling (10)**
Galston Primary School, Galston

# The Unknown Funny Forest

In my dreams every night
I travel to the magic forest where...
Disco dragons dance to awesome disco beats
Wizards whoosh like the wind blowing fiercely
A magical mansion for royalty?

Unknown and unafraid, unicorns rise up and down like a roller coaster
To get to the magical mansion
Amazing astronauts fly through the bright blue sky
I feel like I am flying
Now I am ready to go!

**Ellis Williamson (9)**
Galston Primary School, Galston

# Dino Danger

Standing in the middle of New York,
And a T-rex running, red as a tomato,
Teeth as sharp as hedgehog spikes.
Arms as small as a pencil,
Feet as big as cars.

Screaming like a pirate,
But T-rex is louder.
One yellow eye,
The other one had a death-defying scar.

Cars going one hundred miles per minute,
As the T-rex was in front of me,
And it ate me up.

**Joey McFarlane (9)**
Galston Primary School, Galston

# The Battle Of Britain

Once upon a dream, I was flying my Spitfire,
The sky as black as a black cat on a rug,
Nervously I was about to shoot down my first plane,
Dive and down we flew like a bullet out of a gun.

The battle had begun,
Starting to shoot down Messerschmitt Bf 109s,
Me and my wingman as awesome as an actress,
Flew in hot pursuit of a bomber,
Justice at last for all of us.

**John Stebbings (9)**
Galston Primary School, Galston

# When The Storm Started

When the storm started,
The clouds cried like a baby,
The sardines swam as fast as light,
A great white gobbled up a fish.

When the storm started,
The water roared like a lion,
The lightning growled like a wolf,
The whale whistled like the wind.

When the storm ended,
The ship sank
I woke up and realised it was just a dream.

**Jamie Downie (9)**
Galston Primary School, Galston

# Untitled

When I had a good dream,
I felt like I was on a plane going to Tenerife.
I played on the slides all day long,
Then my mum and dad went to get some breakfast.
I had some eggs and some toast.
My mum had the same,
And my dad had a drink of Coca-Cola.
Then we went back to the water park.
After dinner, I went to bed.

**Niamh Murray (9)**
Galston Primary School, Galston

# Sweetland

In my head every night,
Magical fairies dancing, like twinkling lights,
On bright colourful clouds,
In pranced a beautiful, colourful unicorn,
With a sparkly rainbow mane.
They took me to an amazing, delightful, joyful sweet land,
Where they taught me how to fly like a butterfly.
I felt as brilliant as a superstar!

**Effie McCutcheon (9)**
Galston Primary School, Galston

# The Magical World Of Surprise

In my head, it's a world of surprise.
When I open my eyes, I am shocked.
I am in the land of flowers, as beautiful as a shiny seashell.

In a beautiful land far away,
A beautiful land filled with flowers.
I feel excited, mixed emotions like happiness.
All I smell are flowers, like cupcakes.

**Ellie-Máe Haining (9)**
Galston Primary School, Galston

# The Wilderness

Beautiful water, rushing down a hillside.
Trees sneezing as the leaves blow off.
The scorching sun blazing down on the rainforest animals as they climb the trees, searching for food all day
Elegant swans in the river eating the fish for dinner.
All the babies share the land and the swans get the leftovers.

**Kian Anderson (9)**
Galston Primary School, Galston

# My Dream Life

**M** y dream job is a beautician and own my own shop.
**Y** es, I want two kids, preferably two girls.

**D** reaming for this to happen one day.
**R** emembering to love them with all my heart.
**E** ating in a fancy restaurant with my family.
**A** bsolutely loving my shop and my job.
**M** y dream is to have a big house, two daughters and a really cute dog.

**L** iving in a really big fancy house near the beach.
**I** remember I used to dream about unicorns dancing on rainbows.
**F** or this life to happen, I have to work hard.
**E** very time I dream, it's about having a family.

**Indie-Skye Adams (10)**
Malvern Primary School, Belfast

# The Champions League Final Dreams

I could see a Champions League Final,
And Liverpool was playing against Man United, their rival.
I was in Anfield where the match was happening,
And I was among the fans, who were shouting.

If Liverpool won, I would be very happy,
But if Man United won, it would be very nasty.
The match kicked off and the game started,
But after the first half, I was very broken-hearted.

Rashford and Garnacho scored,
And then I was feeling very bored.
But me feeling broken-hearted and bored didn't last long,
Because Mo Salah scored a hat-trick and I started singing a song,

Liverpool won the Champions League,
Now Liverpool have to focus on winning the Premier League.
I opened my eyes and realised that this was not real or true,
Now, I need to get ready to go to school, very soon.

**Antony Joby (11)**
Malvern Primary School, Belfast

# My Dreams

I have my dream house overlooking the sea,
Having loads of fun, even though it's just me.
I work from my shed,
But it's fine, I still get paid!
People call me a make-up artist,
But if I don't have some on myself I look like a beast.
I can do your nails,
If you need to lift a veil,
I'll do your hair,
If you feel a bit bare,
I will do your eyelashes,
If you want flash, flash, flash,
Then I'll go to bed, just like that!

**Lily Green (10)**
Malvern Primary School, Belfast

# The Haunted House

**N** ight comes quick,
**I** head to the beach and end up at a haunted house,
**G** hosts and ghouls float freely around me,
**H** igh-pitched squeals break the remainder of the window,
**T** errifying red eyes stare at me,
**M** inute after minute I feel like I'm being watched,
**A** tall man starts to follow me,
**R** un, he starts to close in on me,
"**E** ve, wake up" my mum saves me from the nightmare.

**Eve Harris (10)**
Malvern Primary School, Belfast

# 21st Premier League

I can see the goal mouth welcoming my overhead kick.
Man Utd fans scream
*Wow!*

I can hear Man Utd fans chanting my name
I also hear Liverpool fans screaming in anger

I can smell victory and Liverpool's defeat

I taste a bangers and mash

I touch the grass while knee-sliding to heaven
After scoring... what a day!

**Ethan Huston (10)**
Malvern Primary School, Belfast

# Dreamland

**D** uring the night when I close my eyes, I go into a magical land.
**R** emembering the fairies gathering up their fairy dust.
**E** xciting parties waiting for me.
**A** mazing fresh smells.
**M** arvellous cupcakes, sweets and food.
**S** oon enough, we have to say goodbye, as it is nearly morning.

**Maisie Butler (9)**
Malvern Primary School, Belfast

# In My Dreams

**D** reams happen when I am sleeping
**R** emembering is hard
**E** verything is quiet when I sleep
**A** nything is possible in a dream
**M** ainly a dream is a world of your imagination
**S** leeping takes me into a new world!

**Riley Gray (11)**
Malvern Primary School, Belfast

# A Nightmare

When I go to sleep
It looks like an abandoned theme park,
It smells like rotten tree bark,
It sounds like pure silence in the dark,
It feels like rusty metal,
It tastes like dead bugs and jaggy nettles.

**Lukas Darragh Stewart (9)**
Malvern Primary School, Belfast

# In My Dream I'm A Footballer

I travel the world to different pitches
Some pitches are as green as grass
The fans scream like a car screeching from a bank robbery
When the final whistle blows
I wake up!

**Ethan O'Hara (11)**
Malvern Primary School, Belfast

# The Upside-Down World

When I go to sleep and close my eyes,
I see a world of horrid despise.
I hear something running at me,
And he sounds so angry.

**Jacob Scott (10)**
Malvern Primary School, Belfast

# The Snow Kingdom

Once upon a time at the peaks of Mount Creature
Was a very snowy kingdom with a lot of cute features.
Some of which are tall
Some of which are small
But the cutest one of the lot
Is the snow pony who can trot
One day I climbed the mountain
With my pet snowy owl, Fountain
We got to the peak quite fast
So we could set up our tent at last
We met all the creatures of the forest
And then we met the ones that were modest
One windy day a snowstorm blew
But then it grew, grew and grew
I tried to save the animals from the storm
But the hero was the bear with the thorn
He dug us a warm cosy cave
Before we had to meet our grave
The storm blew away at long last
But the day wasn't done so fast
We still had a party to celebrate that day
For Bear who was the hero of our very long day.

**Alicja McLean (10)**
Mobile Play In Action, Airdrie

# Magic Flowers

As I fell asleep on a Sunday
I thought I had a fun day
I played with my best friends
They all follow the latest trends
But that night, I had a dream
I felt so weird that I could scream
I was in a field full of flowers
But I made them float; I have powers

My favourite flower is the daisy
When I saw them, I almost went crazy
I saw poppies, lilies, roses and more
Then a poppy opened its mouth and did a big roar
I saw a lily looking at me
Then it grew wings and flew around while buzzing like a bee
But then my dream came to a stop early
And then I got to sleep, so I'm ready for Monday.

**Holly Moffat (11)**
Mobile Play In Action, Airdrie

# Love

I just need some time to think.
I'm in the bathroom, crying in the sink,
While I'm trying to call you over,
Though I'm tryna get over, over, over.

*Rap:*
I'm thinking of the highs and lows,
Tryna call you when I'm alone.
Miles and miles, I'll be home.
Crying and crying even more.
The thing is, I'm in love,
Just like a dove.
Love, just like a dove.
Falling in love over again.

*Rap:*
I've been thinking of crying and crying,
Tryna get over.
I'm not dying, not dying.
Am I falling in love,
Like a dove?

**Keeva Cowan (9)**
Mobile Play In Action, Airdrie

# Bright, Bright Stars

In this massive Milky Way
There is one thing you should see
There are bright stars, bright stars

Come and follow me
And you will soon see
All the bright stars, bright stars

An astronaut in space
Flies in a spaceship called The Age
Next to the bright stars, bright stars

Space has more to see
Open your eyes and you will see
Just listen to me

A monkey has been to space
I wonder what was his expression on his face
Seeing the bright stars, bright stars

The stars are cool
Don't be a fool
And just look at the bright stars.

**Chloe Longridge (10)**
Mobile Play In Action, Airdrie

# The Demon House

My friends and I were playing tennis.
Then, we dropped our ball.
I ran after it, then I saw a new house;
It was enormous!
I knew the person wouldn't want me to come in,
So I climbed to the roof and went through the loft window.
I saw a giant sword; I grabbed it!
Then, there was a strange boy,
Entirely covered in black except for his eyes,
That were white.
He chased me around
But then he opened his mouth
And started to fly toward me.
Then I ran and grabbed a torch
And held it in front of me.
Then I hit the boy with the sword
And he disappeared.

**Max Murray (9)**
Mobile Play In Action, Airdrie

# The Crazy Poem

Poppies blow row one row
Taking on guards
To see us blow
So out of breath
We laugh and flow
Live, laugh, love
We're so old
Wrinkly but young
Serious but fun!
Weird but silly
Feel like I'm frilly
So full
Feel like a bull
In a pool
So cool
Like a rose
In its pose
Singing and ringing
Louder than a bird singing
All the bells are dinging
Like a dog
Whipping, leaping and sweeping.

**Emmy Armitage (9)**
Mobile Play In Action, Airdrie

# My Mum

Love, love is my mum.
My mum is fun to be with.
My mum is the best and she makes me feel no fret.
She hugs and she kisses and she says she always misses.
My mum is the bracelet
That always stays on my arm and she is no harm.
My mum is the whole of my heart and she is my favourite art.
Her beauty is like a rose that never peels off.
She is the only mum I will always love
And she is my favourite person ever.

**Stephanie Stewart (10)**
Mobile Play In Action, Airdrie

# Dragon

**D** ragons are majestic creatures,
**R** adiant with mythical features,
**A** ncient creatures that have lived for long,
**G** one without a trace, not even a bone,
**O** nce dead, not even an egg on a ledge was found,
**N** one were found because they were slain, and their bones were taken away.

**Gavin Roberts (10)**
Mobile Play In Action, Airdrie

# The Bad And Good

Unicorns flying,
Dinosaurs roaring,
Fairies dancing,
There are some things I want to see.
Footballers fighting,
Dragons killing,
Dancers falling,
These are some things I don't want to see.
There are bad things I don't want to see and good things I do want to see.

**Thea Roscoe (9)**
Mobile Play In Action, Airdrie

# Pink Dream

I put my head on my pillow,
Wait... Where am I?
It's actually pretty here,
I can see blossom trees in the distance,
The blossom trees are the same colour as cotton candy,
The grass feels like wool,
The sky is as blue as the sea on a globe,
I walk forward, and with each step I take, I get -
Higher and higher until I come to a stop!
Oh no, I'm falling, arghh!
*Bang!*
I land with a crash,
Marshmallow clouds dance in the wind,
Yummy sun as bright as a light,
Toy owl as loud as a trumpet,
But I hear a faint voice saying wake up,
But only then did I realise it was a dream.

**Bella Beehan (9)**
Newbridge-On-Wye Church in Wales School, Newbridge-On-Wye

# Untitled

I was upside down in Dreamland,
The sheep, cows and horses eat clouds,
It's down that makes the human realise it's upside down in Dreamland,
Houses are made of foods,
I hear a faint sounds telling me to wake up,
It's school time only then do I realise,
It is a dream.

I realise some dreams are scary like nightmares,
I had already had it was like real life and true,
I woke up I was like scared because it was dark everywhere,
I was looking for my little brother when I couldn't find him,
I realised he was with my mum,
Now I was cooling down, but it was too scary.

**Jameela Cameela Akyaw (9)**
Newbridge-On-Wye Church in Wales School, Newbridge-On-Wye

# Doughnuts And Chocolate

I put my head on a pillow and fall asleep,
The sky is white with pink clouds made of cotton candy doughnuts,
And it is raining doughnuts,
The ground is as bright as the sun,
And the flowers are dancing while it's raining doughnuts,
Then a big doughnut comes,
*Bang! Boom!*
The doughnuts explode everywhere,
The big doughnut stops the raining doughnuts,
There's a slide made out of chocolate,
With a chocolate swimming pool,
With a float made out of doughnuts,
Then I hear a faint sound in the distance,
Telling me to wake up,
Then I realise, it was only a dream.

**Luna Kezze (8)**
Newbridge-On-Wye Church in Wales School, Newbridge-On-Wye

# Untitled

It's upside down in Dreamland,
There's a picture of cats in the clouds,
Snow comes out of the ground, and it's rainbow coloured,
People float up into the air to get to their cars.
The cars go *boooom!*
The houses are made of water with fish floating around.
Farms are as small as a school.
The animals are as small as a fish,
Mountains are covered in pencils,
Dogs have swimming costumes on them, and they are on skateboards.
Beds are made of cheese pizza,
And when you wake up, you are covered in sauce.

**Caitlyn Watling (7)**
Newbridge-On-Wye Church in Wales School, Newbridge-On-Wye

# The Space Adventure

I put my head on the pillow and *bang!*
The rocket blasted off to space
The sky was as black as a shadow
It was as hot as fire up at space
The stars started smiling down at me
The alien was as green as grass
A rocket zoomed past my face
The moon was as circular as a ball
And far away in the distance,
I could see a black hole with animals jumping out
Suddenly, the moon started falling down, down, down,
*Plop!*
The moon was on the floor
But then I realised it was just a dream!

**Freya Hobbs (8)**
Newbridge-On-Wye Church in Wales School, Newbridge-On-Wye

# Wondrous World Of Dreams

*Bang! Boom!* Fireworks go zooming around the place
What in the world?
My cat Tiddles is... talking.
White and dark chocolate is covering the floor.
My cat is wearing a clown suit.
Zip dreams are zooming like lightning.
I have just seen I am an alien
My hair is blue and green
And I can hardly see my arms...
I have five of them.
The sun is saying,
"I am very happy today."
I hear a faint voice in the distance saying,
"Wake up you twit, it is time for school."

**Freyja Hounsome (8)**
Newbridge-On-Wye Church in Wales School, Newbridge-On-Wye

# My Very Own Unique Dream

I put my head on the pillow and...
I was upside down in
What looked like a dreamland!
Flamingos floated around the sky like clouds,
The trees of cotton candy danced in the wind,
Llamas floated up into the sky,
Like inflated balloons going up and up!
The Boba Tea River flowed peacefully
Under the fading sunset.
*Whoosh*, went the llamas slowly
Floating up into the sky.
Suddenly, I heard a faint voice,
Saying, "Wake up,"
Only then did I realise, it was only a dream.

**Evie Millard (9)**
Newbridge-On-Wye Church in Wales School, Newbridge-On-Wye

# Water World Adventures

A world around me,
Pink, green, blue and black,
One happy castle, one sad castle,
The name of this place is Water World.
It's flooded and upside down,
In Water World, there are three waterfalls
One yellow, one orange, one black.
People fly up and say, "Whee!"
All the food screams except cotton candy.
It's the best, like Mrs Butters,
I am living the best life,
Then I hear a faint shout saying, "Wake up!"
It was just a dream.

**Efa Allison (8)**
Newbridge-On-Wye Church in Wales School, Newbridge-On-Wye

# Untitled

I put my head on the pillow,
And saw a land of my own,
With football stadiums made of cotton candy,
And seats made of marshmallows,
And people shouted whee!
Beautiful stars shone in the sky,
I won the Ballon d'Or,
And it was made of vanilla ice cream,
And sunflowers were made of mac 'n' cheese,
And bananas were the banana sweets,
And cars were made of Weetabix,
People were in Ronaldo shorts and Messi shirts.

**Ralph Smith (7)**
Newbridge-On-Wye Church in Wales School, Newbridge-On-Wye

# Loud Dream Land

I put my head on the pillow
I awake, and I am in a world that is in my head
Millions of rats dancing in the wind
*Boom!* A bomb goes off every hour like Big Ben
People float on pizza slices that taste of pepperoni pizza
They say, "Wow," waving their arms
Talking cats are singing "La, la, la, la, la, la"
In disappointment, I say, "Oh, it was only a dream."

**Teddy Smith (8)**
Newbridge-On-Wye Church in Wales School, Newbridge-On-Wye

# Untitled

I put my head on my pillow in Dreamland,
The sky is as blue as the sea,
The grass is as colourful as a rainbow,
Clouds are as fluffy as cotton candy,
Houses are made of cake, *yum yum!*
Dogs are flying in the blue sky,
Sitting on a gaming controller,
In Dreamland, there are birds the colour of a rainbow,
And the cats have goggles on while going down a slide, *whee!*

**Max Prosser (8)**
Newbridge-On-Wye Church in Wales School, Newbridge-On-Wye

# My Dream Land

In Dream Land, it is upside down.

The floor is made out of a carpet that smells like sweets.

There is a chocolate river.

Candy canes as street lamps.

The clouds are made out of cotton candy.

Everyone jumps on them and eats them. When they jump on the clouds, they go, "Whee!"

Dolly sweets are falling and dancing through the sky.

**Caiden Thomas (7)**
Newbridge-On-Wye Church in Wales School, Newbridge-On-Wye

# Once Upon A Dream

There were giant penguins floating in the light blue sea
With flying polar bears in the sky.
Pufferfish floating up in the air like a balloon,
Walrusses sliding around on ice
Flying ice around, floating in the air like icebergs
Crashing into stuff in the wind,
Golden snowflakes falling down from the air,
Lions rolling around in the snow made of copper.

**Archie Cullum (8)**
Newbridge-On-Wye Church in Wales School, Newbridge-On-Wye

# Untitled

A snow mountain stood in my way,
The cold is colder than Mount Everest,
The water is darker than a whiteboard pen,
I heard the fish are redder than the red dragon,
The clouds are made out of pasta,
The human pastels dance in a Man U kit,
They sing Dance Monkey,
The fish dance like Michael Jackson,
I heard a big sound,
Just then I woke up.

**Finn Samuel (8)**
Newbridge-On-Wye Church in Wales School, Newbridge-On-Wye

# I Put My Head On The Pillow

I was in a place I had never been in before.
It had clouds for beds.
When you jumped in the water, it made a splash!
People were doing the Griddy.
They were in Al-Nassr and Manchester United Football kits
Chocolate houses stood proudly
The people were made of gingerbread
I jumped twice and I was flying.
I flew down then I woke up.

**Regan Christie-Rees (8)**
Newbridge-On-Wye Church in Wales School, Newbridge-On-Wye

# I Love Sleep

*Bang!*
I am falling on a bouncy castle.
I look around and see cats in clown suits,
People are made from sweets,
The flowers are too.
Cows sing like Michael Jackson,
It rains food like fish and chips,
And the clouds are made from cheese.
Then I hear my dad sing,
"Wake up!"
I realise it was a dream!

**Lily Waters (8)**
Newbridge-On-Wye Church in Wales School, Newbridge-On-Wye

# Imagination Land

I fell asleep and then my imagination went wild,
Donkeys were doing backflips and frontflips,
Fish were playing the drums,
Birds were singing never gonna give you up,
*Boom!* A bomb landed near a building,
The ocean was frogspawn,
Dad said, "Wake up, you're late for school!"

**Oliver Jones (9)**
Newbridge-On-Wye Church in Wales School, Newbridge-On-Wye

# Untitled

I fell fast asleep and...
Gargantuan green pencils stand
As tall as the Empire State Building
Tap water goes *drip, drip, drip.*
Seals dance around the air,
Like balloons.
The floor is made of hard gold.
*Crash!* I wake up on the floor.
Then I realise it was a dream.

**John Meredith (8)**
Newbridge-On-Wye Church in Wales School, Newbridge-On-Wye

# The Magical Unicorn

When I fell asleep,
I saw the most magical dream,
Of sparkles that danced,
Rainbow unicorns with sparkly wings,
The unicorns were dancing and spinning,
The mane on the unicorn was rainbow and sparkly,
Wow!
It was like a fairy tale,
I woke up and it was just a dream.

**Paige Baynham (7)**
Newbridge-On-Wye Church in Wales School, Newbridge-On-Wye

# Untitled

A naughty frog is seen hopping,
The sky is black like coal,
I play football for Man U in darkish red shirt,
Flying cows whizz past,
Singing cockerels, hallelulia!
Drums hit like bombs,
Huge double-deckers as tall as a giant.
I woke up and it was a dream.

**William Savage Samuel (8)**
Newbridge-On-Wye Church in Wales School, Newbridge-On-Wye

# Untitled

In Dreamland there are two dimensions
Dreamland is a million years old
And the dimensions are called
The Cotton Candy and the Black Dimension.
Then I realised I was in a dream loop.

**Aneurin Edwards (7)**
Newbridge-On-Wye Church in Wales School, Newbridge-On-Wye

# The Enchanted Forest

In the woods so green where dreams take flight,
An enchanted forest sparked in the moonlight.

Happy fairies started to dance so sweet,
With colourful butterflies in a magical feast.

Trees whispered secrets to all the animals,
With their branches balancing on the waterfalls.

Listen closely you can hear the wind sing,
In the Enchanted Forest where dreams belong.

**Victoire Deconinck (8)**
Our Lady Of Victories RC Primary School, London

# Dream

**D** reams are good, thoughtful ideas for both day and night.
**R** emember your dreams can always happen, but only if you try.
**E** very child and adult will have good or bad dreams.
**A** nd what do you dream about?
**M** y dream is to be flying in the sky with unicorns, and swimming with dolphins.

**Romy Treguer (8)**
Our Lady Of Victories RC Primary School, London

# The Weather Is Changing

The moon is like a diamond in the night sky.
A jewel shining in the moon's bright light beauty.
A beautiful diamond, enchanting the heavens and the milky galaxy.
A beautiful and enchanting diamond moon as beautiful as a rose.
A sparkling moon, smiling back at me and precious to my heart.
The sun is glowing.
Hotness shines down on my beautiful face; first, a sprinkle, then a pouring.
Watching rain is never boring.
Clouds of grey.
Refreshing shower sequences.
All of the thirsty flowers' sparkling icicles that had once been water.
Now, the pond has been covered in sparkly powder.
Snow on the meadow, snow on the ground, and snow prances and dances;
While it shines beautifully in the air, the wind blows around like confetti.

**Amelia Henners (10)**
Our Lady Queen Of Peace Catholic Primary School, Litherland

# Escaped The Dark

In my dreams every night,
I see flames of fire dancing around the trees.
I run as fast as I can,
With a delightful smile on my face.
Suddenly when I got closer and closer,
My delightful smile faded away.
As I turned back, I was lost, before you knew it,
I saw a huge monster chasing me.
As I ran I felt my heart fall apart,
I felt my tears trickle off my skin,
As I felt really angry,
But something unexpected happened,
I turned back with all my courage and anger,
Suddenly, the monster ran away from me
And disappeared into thin air.
And that's when I knew I could escape the dark.

**Michelle Etuk (10)**
Our Lady Queen Of Peace Catholic Primary School, Litherland

# Up, Up We Go

One day me and my friend died,
We ended up in Heaven and we flew high.
What did we see? A magic cat,
It made a fish appear with its hat!
We saw a little XL bully,
It wore a scarf oh so woolly.
There was a tiny little frog,
It sat on a very short log.
What I saw next was really shocking,
You won't believe me when I say this was a very tragic day.
What I saw behind the log,
Was another tiny frog.
That was my friend, you didn't believe it,
But then the water started to glimmer and gleam.
Then I woke up and found out it was all a dream!

**Millie Hannan (9)**
Our Lady Queen Of Peace Catholic Primary School, Litherland

# What Are Dreams Made Of?

Dreams are made of an array of emotions,
Depending on who you are,
So who are you?
You might be a little boy,
Who had dreams of losing his favourite toy,
Or a girl that got stuck in a twirl.
But a dream that we've all had,
Is a frightening dream.
When someone is falling or a slender crooked figure,
Or are you in a desolate land?
So ancient vines are entangling the windows and light,
As you enter through the mossy window,
You spot a creature that scares you,
And you wake up.

**Elisha Odeh (10)**
Our Lady Queen Of Peace Catholic Primary School, Litherland

# Dreams Of A Footballer

As players walk onto the pitch,
Hoping for that big win,
Dreaming of how many goals each of them can score,
Just to hear that crowd roar.

Footballers dreaming of getting that ball,
Running across the pitch just to hear that crowd roar.

Footballers dreaming of wearing that kit,
Whatever the weather,
Whatever the day,
It doesn't matter one bit.

My heart and soul is football,
Forever it will be,
Putting on that shiny shirt,
Will always fill me with glee.

**Pippa King (10)**
Our Lady Queen Of Peace Catholic Primary School, Litherland

# Library

In a library of books, I saw
Three beautifully gleaming books
Waiting for me to read them.

In a library of books, I saw
Six friendly librarians
Helping people find the books
That they wanted to read.

In a library of books, I saw
Nine silent bookworms
Reading their books.

In a library of books, I saw
Twelve storybooks for little kids
Lying on their shelf
Whilst children looked around.

**Sophie Dears (9)**
Our Lady Queen Of Peace Catholic Primary School, Litherland

# Candy Land

Once upon a time, in a world of imagination,
Take my hand as we enter Candy Land,
A place of wonder,
A place of joy,
A place that everyone can enjoy.

It is so sweet,
You will never want to leave,
Because you can believe how wonderful Candy Land is.

**Ava Devlin (9)**
Our Lady Queen Of Peace Catholic Primary School, Litherland

# Everyone Has A Dream To Achieve

Everyone has a dream to achieve,
Everyone has a skill to do,
Everyone has a goal for a sport,
Everyone reaches out for the dream,
Everyone uses teamwork for their dream,
Some people don't realise they have a dream.

**Evie Hughes (10)**
Our Lady Queen Of Peace Catholic Primary School, Litherland

# Dreamer

Last night, I went to bed,
Went to rest for the long day ahead.
I went to sleep and saw a dude,
And to my surprise, he was running around nude!

Then, all of a sudden, I teleported somewhere new
And everything was beautiful, if I am being true.
A dragon flew past me, "Full speed ahead!"
Supposedly, that was what the girl said.
Follow me, you won't regret,
And in the blink of an eye, I was riding her dragon pet!

We ventured off into a magical wood;
I would revisit it if I could.
And then we played, until sunset
And she told me I hadn't seen the best bit yet.

As she said, "Follow me!"
She took me up to the highest tree.
The sun was huge and had an orangey glow
And that was a moment I couldn't let go.

I woke up ready for the day,
But not letting the dream fade away.
And when I got home, all cosy and warm,
I got ready for my new dream to transform

**Lottie Cole (11)**
Rice Lane Primary School, Liverpool

# Untitled

The morning light shone across the ocean,
It glimmered.
The window opened
And the smell of the morning woke me up.
I felt like a rose on a hot sunny day.
In the yard, the feathers flew around my head,
The butterflies flew around me snoring.
Before I knew it a shadow came, it went dark.
I woke up on the floor.
I didn't know what to do.
I stumbled and tripped over a tree root;
My knees, overgrown and bloody.
I saw a wizard upon the jet-black sky.
Was I hallucinating?
The eye looked at me with horror
As I cried all the way through the haunting woods.
The risk of following this path was in my hand.
There were woods as I crept closer and closer to whatever was in the darkness,
It crawled closer as I went pale,
My mouth went dry and it went dark.
I shook the thought out that was in my head,
It went pitch-black.

**Harriet Coady-Taylor (9)**
Rice Lane Primary School, Liverpool

# I Dream Of A Nightmare

Once I had a nightmare that was also a dream,
It was full of happy moments but also made me scream.
My dream began with me playing football in front of the Kop,
But then an axe man appeared and I knew I was in for the chop.

I drove away quickly in my brand-new Ferrari,
But then I ended up in the Lion's Den at Knowsley Safari.
I turned the car around and headed into town,
I then went into Zara and came across a scary clown!

I grew a pair of wings and flew away fast,
But then I fell from the air and ended up in a full-body cast!
What will I dream of tonight and tomorrow?
Will it be joyful, or full of sorrow...

But always remember dreams and nightmares are just in your head,
You'll always wake up, safely in bed.

**Sofia Tyrrell (10)**
Rice Lane Primary School, Liverpool

# Imagination

**I** magination starts with thoughts in your head.
**M** ainly they come alive whilst lying in bed,
**A** ngels, astronauts, fairies with crowns,
**G** alloping and twirling around fantasy town.
**I** nside a cave lives a queen and a king,
**N** aughty children have hidden the golden ring,
**A** cross the sky, a rainbow slide,
**T** ime flies like a fast swirly ride,
**I** cicles like lollipops hang from the trees,
**O** ctopuses glide and swim in the breeze.
**N** ow you need to cherish these thoughts in your mind.

**Phoebe Edwards (10)**
Rice Lane Primary School, Liverpool

# Kangaroo Across The Country

Kangaroo across the country,
With a joey in her pouch
All snug, warm and cosy like her own little house.

Kangaroo across the country,
In the blazing, beaming sun,
Where they hop about all day long,
But you will never see them run.

Kangaroo across the country,
They sleep the whole day away,
They wake by night to graze,
And have a little play.

Kangaroo across the country,
From a place down under,
Loving life in Australia,
What's it like there?
I will always wonder.

**Paul Atkinson (10)**
Rice Lane Primary School, Liverpool

# A Strange Sleep

Last night was exhausting,
And my energy I was resourcing.
So I put my head down,
With a big, nasty frown,
And started to dream till the morning.

I dreamt of a potato,
That turned me into fries,
And then all of a sudden,
I started to fly!

Next, I was a bat
Hanging upside down,
Looking around,
Looking at the town.

But don't forget about the dream.
I was stuck in a submarine,
Laughing at all the sharks swimming by,
The fish, the squid and the octopi.

**Mya-Rose Rice (11)**
Rice Lane Primary School, Liverpool

# A Dancer's Passion

How elegant dancers are,
Their turns, their swirls.
Dancers have an amazing passion,
Their jumps, their leaps.
I love to see them on stage,
With all their hair and make-up done.
Their costumes shimmer on stage,
They're that pretty they look like dolls.
They flip their hair and twirl,
Oh how pretty they are.
What a pity only one can win,
Who will get a golden medal?
I wish it would be me,
The contest may start, ladies,
Let's see who wins!

**Myla Woodward (8) & Isla**
Rice Lane Primary School, Liverpool

# Dreaming, Dreaming

I fall asleep with a big goodnight,
I rise up to the morning light,
But I realise it's just a sight,
I suddenly realise, I am still asleep.

Let this be the sleep of the deeper sea,
But below the sea, I am above the sky,
As I see a dream that waits for me.

I open the door to open up to the world I see,
The night falls, the dreams awake as I drift off.
The door to leave, open the gate,
I see the dreams,
I've never seen a night like this.

**M Patrick (10)**
Rice Lane Primary School, Liverpool

# Flying Dancers And Flying Gymnasts

Dancers fly,
Gymnasts fly,
But who is better?
Dancers fly by jumping,
Gymnasts fly by flipping,
The rivalry starts,
Some dance academies do aero,
Some don't,
None know,
Who is better?
Dance has multiple styles,
Gymnastics has multiple events,
Both have girl and boy events,
More styles for dance,
Dance has one point,
Gymnastics zero,
But still three more rounds,
Make-up?
Gymnastics nothing,
Dancers a lot.

**Cali Gray (9) & Connie Corker (9)**
Rice Lane Primary School, Liverpool

# A Gymnast

A gymnast is a working person,
So intrigued by what they do,
So elegant in the way they move,
And difficult in the way they groove.

A gymnast flies high like a bird in the sky.
Gymnasts have perfect posture, not like me or you.
A gymnast is flexible and loose, unlike dancers.
Gymnastics is their passion, a cool thing to do.

That's their passion, don't take it away!
So join gymnastics today!

**Sophie Cunliffe (9) & Emily McDermott (8)**
Rice Lane Primary School, Liverpool

# Clowns

Roses are red,
Violets are blue,
If you think clowns are creepy,
I've got a poem for you.

Clowns, clowns everywhere,
The people who scream,
The people who scare,
Sometimes they come into my dreams
And make me have frightening screams.

I have nightmares,
I have dreams,
Is it the clowns that cause these screams?

**Olivia Wood (10)**
Rice Lane Primary School, Liverpool

# The Unicorn Of Love

In my dreams, I see the unicorn of love,
Starlight's her name,
Just like Cupid, people fall in love,
All across the world the love squad go,
On the special day, Valentine's Day,
They spread their love,
But not for Misty, who spreads misery for all.

**Darcy Teer (9)**
Rice Lane Primary School, Liverpool

# My Gymnastic's Dream

With a leap, I can touch the sky,
In the gym, my dreams do fly,
I practise my skills on the vault and beam,
To never give up as hard as it seems,
The competition has finished, but what is my fate?
I closed my eyes and heard, "First place!"

**Poppy Hart (8)**
Rice Lane Primary School, Liverpool

# Rainbow

**R** ipe oranges
**A** cross the trees
**I** n a land far far away
**N** obody can see, no one but me
**B** lissful sounds of the waves
**O** h what a beautiful dream
**W** hy do they have to end?

**Quinn Pruden (10)**
Rice Lane Primary School, Liverpool

# Holidays

**H** appy days
**O** n the beach
**L** ots of fun
**I** ce cream all round
**D** ays after days
**A** way from home on
**Y** ellow majestic
**S** and all day.

**Marley Dainton King (9)**
Rice Lane Primary School, Liverpool

# The Space Monster

In my sleep every time,
My space monster appears in my eyes.
He is bright and blue, and a giant,
And he is very, very quiet.

One day, as I get into bed,
I realise my space monster isn't ahead.
So I search and search and search,
But it just doesn't work.

I ask the other space monsters where he is,
But when I ask, some just carry on eating their chocolate bars.

As I near the end of my dream,
I feel like I want to scream.
Then a space monster comes to me,
And says my space monster is on a holiday near the sea.
He says he will come next year,
But to me, it feels like he just disappeared.

**Maria Sobin (9)**
St Andrew's CE Junior School, Burnham-On-Sea

# Dancing Upon The Stars

I lie awake in my bed at night,
Waiting for that special flight.
I close my eyes and suddenly I see
A fairy hovering over me.
She sprinkles dust here and there,
Suddenly, there are stars everywhere!
I've been whooshed away to outer space
Where I can see my sister's face.
We dance around the glowing lights,
The moon and stars are shining bright.
We laugh and dance the night away
Hoping it will never be day.
I open my eyes and there I'm led,
All tucked up in my cosy bed.

**Laicey Fowler (9)**
St Andrew's CE Junior School, Burnham-On-Sea

# My Fairy Dream...

Whilst I lay cosy in my bed,
I dreamt of fairies flying above my head.
Their wings sparkled like gold,
Their magic wand had secrets untold.
The forest they lived in was enchanted and special,
They played in the flowers, trees and nettles.
Their little homes had tiny wooden doors,
Here they baked delicious cakes and more.
My favourite fairy is Belle, she is the queen,
Her beautiful green and gold dress shines in my dream.

**Maddison Davies (7)**
St Andrew's CE Junior School, Burnham-On-Sea

# The Dream

My dream is to be a ballerina, to curl and swirl.
To be on stage and not to be afraid.
I had the chance to do my dance,
So I wore my shoes to dance the blues,
And I had the best moves.
I had good turnout,
But sometimes I did burn out.
I had a passion,
That was not just a fashion.
It was a love that would go on forever
Through every endeavour.
I would not bail, I would beam,
Because that was my dream.

**Freya Jeffries (9)**
St Andrew's CE Junior School, Burnham-On-Sea

# Magical Ways

**M** y dreams are always simple, but this one's something!
**A** magical door appears in a forest, bright and blue,
**G** athering my strength, I open the door.
**I** see a giant white elephant with an old man riding on his back,
**"C** ome here!" he shouts.
**A** nxiously, I approach.
**L** eaning close, he says, "You will learn my magical ways!"

## Morgana Cameron (9)
St Andrew's CE Junior School, Burnham-On-Sea

# Class A3

Once there was a school,
With colourful pictures on the wall,
Class A3 had a fox called Rox,
Who was sitting in a cardboard box,
A cat called Bat,
Loved wearing a golden hat,
A frog called Tog,
Was always reading a book called Zog.

One day, they went to the swimming pool,
Where Rox forgot his cardboard box,
Bat lost his golden hat,
And Tog turned into Zog!

**Sofia Hall (8)**
St Andrew's CE Junior School, Burnham-On-Sea

# Lego Life

**L** iving life in a coloured world of blocks,
**E** verlasting hours of adventures, using my imagination,
**G** oing to have so much fun building my creation,
**O** n the sound of my alarm clock, I awake to jump out of bed and find my feet in a Lego clutter. Under my breath, I mutter, "I must put away my Lego life!"

**Fynnley Strange (9)**
St Andrew's CE Junior School, Burnham-On-Sea

# Cara The Cat

Cara the Cat
Saw a rat.
But the rat did not run like the others.

Cara the Cat
Was confused
All the rats ran away when they saw her.

Cara the Cat
Watched:
Instead of running,
Dozens of rats came!

Cara the Cat
Said, "Is this real?"
But... it was all just a dream!

**Frankie Pini (7)**
St Andrew's CE Junior School, Burnham-On-Sea

# Lost In A Town Of Magic!

Lost in a town of magic, lots of things around.
Some things are waiting for them to be found.
Lost in a town of magic, giants scary and bald.
Lost in a town of magic, scary this and scary that,
Scary everything around.
Magic here, magic there, magic everywhere!

**Mabel-Rose Warrilow (9)**
St Andrew's CE Junior School, Burnham-On-Sea

# The Forest Of The Dead

Bewildered in a wood or lost in a maze?
The stag beside me
As threatened as I am.
The wolf-cub has a mind of his own,
Barking at a chewed stick,
But it wasn't what I thought it was.
It was a bone,
Lots of them scattered across the floor.
So we ran until the floor fell in,
Trees crashing,
The stream forming a waterfall
Into a deep, obsidian abyss.
I screamed, the wolf-cub barked in a deafening way,
And the stag, gone.
Was he down the hole, or had he run away?
I heard a splash and then a beckon,
He was down the hole.
I jumped in after him with the obstreperous blackness curling round me.
The darkness faded into a marigold sun,
Then a shadow cast over me and then...
I was awake.

**Charlie Maudsley (10)**
St Joseph's RC Primary School, Hurst Green

# Bake Off Battle

I had a dream last night,
Oh, it filled me with a fright,
I was absolutely rattled,
I was in a Bake Off Battle!
I was going to have to bake,
Waffles in a competition against pancakes,
My reputation was at stake.

I was against Pancake Penny,
Our judge was to be Ballistic Benny,
The battle starts as Benny hits the gong,
Off we go with a dong, dong, dong!

I grabbed a bowl, my ingredients went in,
I was determined that I would win,
But Pancake Penny was going fast,
She was baking in a blast!

There was only two minutes left on the clock,
I was going to have to block
Pancake Penny so she wouldn't win,
Hopefully her pancake would fall in the bin.

I put my waffle on the judge's table,
And stuck my leg out to make Penny unstable,
She was falling and our food combined,
A stranger dessert you'd never find.
So what would be the winning bake?
Benny declared, "It's the panwaff cake!"

**Joe Canty (9)**
St Joseph's RC Primary School, Hurst Green

# Cookie Vs Biscuit

I had a dream last night,
Oh, it was such a sight,
It stayed in my head,
The cookie monster in my bed,
The foe in my dream.
Oh, what could this mean?
My brain was flummoxed,
The biscuit batter mixed,
I flung to the ground,
A cookie went pound,
As it slammed to the ground,
Serene,
Or was it as it seemed...

It was a battle,
Monster vs monster,
Cookie vs biscuit,
An incursion of cookies,
Some raw, some whole,
They were flung at such a speed,
Bombarding me,
With my worst dream,
Cookies like cannonballs,

Biscuits like meteors,
Exploding everywhere,
*Boom! Bang! Crash!*
They went whizzing past my eyes...
And I woke up.

It was such a fright,
But who had won for the night?
Thoughts raced in my brain,
It was a storm full of rain,
Flooding the thoughts on the run,
Who had won?

**Emma McCrea (11)**
St Joseph's RC Primary School, Hurst Green

# Bake Off Battle

I had a dream last night,
Oh boy, it gave me a fright.
I woke up with a pancake head,
Oh, how I wished I'd stayed in bed.

So I got up and went downstairs,
But to my surprise they had moved all the chairs!
It was replaced with a cooking show set-up,
Oh, now I was happy I'd got up.

I was on TV,
But there was one thing I didn't want to see...
It was Waffle Joe, oh no, no!
I really wanted to leave,
but I couldn't believe,
Joe pulled out a waffle,
I pulled out a pancake.
The judge mushed them together
And took a bite.
It was such a sight.
We both won and made a panwaff,
And ate them all, scoff, scoff, scoff.

**Penny Grace Rowland (10)**
St Joseph's RC Primary School, Hurst Green

# Drifting To Dream World

A blanket filled with warmth,
The soft fur, like a hot water bottle,
Azure eyes say I love you,
The tail wagging away serene feelings,
My dog's fur is an extra pillow for my head,
As I drift off to a blissful and soothing sleep.

But in this realm of sleep,
A land with colours,
Colours leaking out,
A land with clouds,
Soft, snow-white clouds,
Nothing had prepared me for this world,
This beguiling place,
This tranquil space,
What a beauty,
But there in front of me was my dog,
Her ears were silky soft,
Her fur was golden like the sun.

As I realised that I was snuggled up in my bed, all warm and cosy.

**Sarah McCrea (11)**
St Joseph's RC Primary School, Hurst Green

# Glorious Cat Haven

**G** leaming skies
**L** ilac, lemon, lapis colours all around me,
**O** chre and orchid,
**R** unning around me.
**I** saw cats, cats, and more cats.
**O** h, I said as I reached down to pet them
**U** p above was a palace
**S** ensational brickwork.

**C** ascading down as a rainbow.
**A** ll the colours were in it,
**T** here was a throne inside the palace.

**H** aving seen this,
**A** ll the feelings rushed through my head.
**V** oracious cats search for food,
**E** mbedded in the throne was where it was.
**N** o, I exclaim as I wake up, I want to stay.

**Samuel Wilkinson (11)**
St Joseph's RC Primary School, Hurst Green

# My Puggy Rainforest

I fall asleep, all warm and cosy,
But all I could think about was leaves,
A sea of sage leaves,
I closed my eyes,
*Boom!*
Rainforest,
Fuschia flowers,
Butterflies like ballet dancers,
My grumpy pug,
No surprise,
Leapt up to a rise,
To avoid the jaguar,
He's really quite wise,
And then the jaguar's there,
Right in front of me,
A tangerine with black stripes,
Above a canopy of mint and emerald leaves,
Swaying in the musty pungent air,
I wish this would never end,
But sadly it did,
I woke up with my pug under my brand-new rug.

**Celia Milligan (10)**
St Joseph's RC Primary School, Hurst Green

# One Dream About Being A Footballer

One dream became the best moment of my life.
I was on the football pitch,
The grass as green as emeralds.
The stadium, pure perfection,
The lights blinding me with happiness and joyful feelings.
I was a professional footballer,
Performing.
The stadium is my stage.

I see the ball,
I see the net.
*Boom!*
I kick the ball,
It flies like a rocket setting off.
It's a shooting star
Heading for goal.
Almost there...
*Goal...*

I woke up with a smile on my face,
But I longed to return
To my dream.

**Harrison Holden (9)**
St Joseph's RC Primary School, Hurst Green

# Untitled

My dream is to dance, but oh,
What a dream,
And what is a dance?
And what does it mean?
Dancing is so much more than it seems.

It is a flower blooming, full of life and movement,
It is wave crashing down onto the shore,
Powerful, rhythmic, mesmerising.
It is a bird in flight,
Graceful, fluid, free.
The crowd roars,
The feeling of euphoria engulfs me.

I hope my dream comes true...

My dream is to dance, but oh,
What a dream,
And what is a dance?
And what does it mean?
Dancing is so much more than it seems.

**Athealia Sumner (11)**
St Joseph's RC Primary School, Hurst Green

# My Dream Is A Beam Of Light

Cyan, azure sea,
Amber, golden sun,
Relaxing in the world of peace.
Like a calming massage, encouraging you to
Become invigorated.
Smelling the salty smell of the sea floating
Through the air, as I felt the smooth snakey
Sand slipping through my fingers.
Waves crashing,
Wind howling,
Dolphins diving,
Boats floating in the formidable mighty ocean.
I heard the tropical birds singing in harmony,
*Kurk-kurk*
The sound of the birds stopped.
Then silence.

I have awoken and the sparkling sapphire seas are no more!

**Fatima Alshahada (10)**
St Joseph's RC Primary School, Hurst Green

# Skating In A Dream

In my dreams I skate,
On the glassy surface of the lake,
A mirror reflecting my contentment.

Behind me, I leave ribbons,
Swirling and engraving,
The ice with patterns galore.

I am on a stage of ice,
The sunset is my spotlight,
The light of the sunset follows my trail,
Am I a ballerina performing on stage?
It feels like it,
My skates are very luminous,
They are so colourful.

Then I see black...
Has my skating session ended?
My mum shouts, "Breakfast is ready!"
Sadly, it was just a dream.

**Daisy Moorby (10)**
St Joseph's RC Primary School, Hurst Green

# Finally Famous

Gold shimmering around us,
Sam and I,
We can't believe it,
What is this place?
I need a clue,
Of course my wish,
It really came true,
We're famous.

A stream meandering through the meadows,
Beautiful sights all around me,
A TV, I pressed a button,
It shot on,
Florence Alwyn, the queen, is being taken,
On holiday by glamorous Charlotte Woods,
I turned the TV off.

"Lucy wake up,"
I woke up,
No,
It was a dream,
Although I had what I needed (love), I was mad.

**Lucy Wilkinson (9)**
St Joseph's RC Primary School, Hurst Green

# The Oak Tree

In my dream, I wake up puzzled and bewildered,
I am in a wood,
All I see are emerald-green leaves,
Swaying in the breeze,
Where am I?
Suddenly, something catches my eye,
A portal of amethyst, azure and marigold,
It is by an oak tree,
The bronze, walnut oak tree has something mysterious about it,
All of a sudden,
I feel the portal bringing me in,
I try to stop it, but I can't,
I am trapped,
I am lost,
Then I feel safe, warm covers over me,
I run home,
After that I am never sleeping again!

**Florence Meadows (10)**
St Joseph's RC Primary School, Hurst Green

# The Amazon Rainforest

I drift off to faraway lands.
A jungle to explore... The Amazon.
Hot and humid.
As the snakes of the jungle slither slowly.
Through the emerald ground.
Overhead there is a swarm of bombarding bugs.
Feasting on the remains of my flesh.
As a jaguar ravenously glares at me.

But then the beauty occurs too.
The raindrops pitter-patter.
Tap dancing on the leaves.
As the trackless unexplored river swishes and sways all day.
The sun leaks through the gaps of the trees.
Like a statue.
Standing still.

**Zach Falencki (9)**
St Joseph's RC Primary School, Hurst Green

# A Nightmare Like No Other

A belligerent monster rears up and roars,
Trapped in a dream,
Lost in the woods,
Trees with faces,
Snarling at me,
Their fingers reach out,
No way out,
No friends close,
Evil wizards in the trees,
What should I do?

A snapping branch,
Out of the dark, a clown comes out,
Followed by spiders,
Legs as sharp as needles,
A nightmare world,
A life like no other.

I'm swallowed by a Kraken,
I wake up with a start,
Monsters lurk in my cupboard,
Until I dream again.

**Bracken James (10)**
St Joseph's RC Primary School, Hurst Green

# The Lost Explorers

One day I was dreaming about
The Amazon rainforest
It was hot and humid
With heat in the air like a burning furnace
The dense canopy a roof of leaves
An evil witch
The growls of predators
A green maze trapping you
This was a suffering, unliveable land

But in this beauty of a landscape
Birds fly by like rainbows dancing from tree to tree
The song of the birds
Harmony in my ears
The rivers, ribbons of water
Waterfalls crashing on the water below
The sound of peace
Hypnotising.

**William Dilworth (9)**
St Joseph's RC Primary School, Hurst Green

# Falling!

I'm falling,
It's horror,
The world's getting closer,
The towering mountains leaving me behind,
Like a car in a race,
The world suddenly encloses,
Surely this is the end,
The earth, a monster, going to swallow me whole,
Thud!
Silence...

I wake up,
My legs and head supported on a cushion,
Was it a dream? No!
My eyes open and someone is there,
A doctor,
I really did fall,
Wait!
I awake once more,
A real moment of bliss,
I realise I'm home.

**Tom McNeela (10)**
St Joseph's RC Primary School, Hurst Green

# Sleep Land Is Here

I am asleep, sleep, sleep,
My mummy brushes my head,
With her finger, finger, finger,
I catch a glimpse of sparkles.

Suddenly, I see, see, see,
Cushions, cushions everywhere,
I wander here,
I wander there,
Softer, softer I drift,
Over there, over there.

Couldn't feel sleepier.

I see a cushion bridge,
It is soft, soft,
I walk, walk over there,
I land, land, land,
Land in the river, I do,
Tuck myself in,
And drift off to sleep, sleep, sleep.

**Grace Elizabeth Hardman (9)**
St Joseph's RC Primary School, Hurst Green

# The Problem

In my dreams every night
I am in deep space on a ship called
Inferno!
With my partner, Red.
All the instruments are going wrong
And the ship is going off course.
Suddenly, the corruption alarm
Goes off. Oh no, not a corruption
From the Nightmare King!
Last time I just disappeared
Into deep space, but there is not
Enough fuel in the engine, so I get
My Disappearing Ray and, *boom!*
The corruption is gone and the ship is fixed.
Let's get back on course.

**Sebastian (9)**
St Joseph's RC Primary School, Hurst Green

# Midnight Frights

I am sitting here at the circus
Waiting
Then, from a puff of magenta smoke
They are there
Heads low, smiling at me
Clowns devoid of humour
The red, painted smiles are sneers
Revealing sharp, treacherous teeth
I run into a dark room
Locking the door
Picturing them in my mind
I fear the worst
They are right behind me
Staring into my soul
I wake up breathing heavily in my bed.

**Ellie Grix (9)**
St Joseph's RC Primary School, Hurst Green

# The Lone, Scary Night

One scary night
Lightning woke me with a fright
I looked under my bed
My legs felt dead
I turned my head and
Saw a monster, who said...
*"I am your worst nightmare!"*
He had tremendous white eyes
And filled my mind with lies
His mouth was filled with razor-sharp teeth
And told me he would always be underneath
Whenever I went to sleep
Ready to haunt my dreams.

**Freddy Jackson (10)**
St Joseph's RC Primary School, Hurst Green

# The Beach

Cerulean sea
Golden sand
Lapis sky
Pristine water
Nothing could take this away from me
Or so I thought...

One thunderclap
It is gone, forever
Of course
Time doesn't persist for long
Junk scattered haphazardly across the land

I woke up in bed, this wasn't true
Hoping this was a dream
Wishing I had not got out of bed
Things much improve

**Alexander Backshall (10)**
St Joseph's RC Primary School, Hurst Green

# A Perfect Night

Up in the clouds
I flew through the night
I passed many stars: brighter than bright
The moon was a diamond
Oh, what a sight!
As I reached out into the darkness...

I found myself back in my bed
And realised it was all in my head.

**Gus Morley (11)**
St Joseph's RC Primary School, Hurst Green

# A Shooting Star's Wish

As I soared over the city I saw,
Children watching and wishing in awe,
"A shooting star!" they say,
Wishing, wondering, praying until the break of day,
Then I come across a broken old shed,
Racked with people but only one bed,
As I glided over,
I saw rich families even with a chauffeur,
Feeling bad I listened to his wish,
"I need food, water and a home. I'll even take a single dish,"
Immediately I got to work,
And I did not shirk,
Now the boy's dad has a great job,
I was so sad by his story, he made me sob,
Happy now my work is done,
I hope the next shooting star can give hope to everyone.

**Evie Champion (10)**
St Martin's School, Bournemouth

# A Stormy Pirate Day

In my dreams,
Bobbing on the colossal, sparkly sea,
Are some pirates being sneaky.

The air feels as hot as a fire,
And the pirates have a desire,
They want treasure,
Lots and lots of treasure.

Drinking all day on the deck,
The pirates suddenly go, "What the heck?"
In the gloomy sky, which is as dark as the Milky Way now,
They can hear thunder go, *pow!*

The sky is now an exploding bomb,
With lightning striking a pirate called Tom,
All of a sudden, it calmed down,
And luckily, no one drowned.

**Martha Callear (10)**
St Martin's School, Bournemouth

# Be Enthralled

The sky is a snuggly quilt of blue
smothering the sky, keeping us safe from space.

The feathery, soft clouds enjoy wafting
over the brilliant blue ocean.

The sky screams out in pain
as Mount Everest's razor-sharp tip,
punches a hole through the middle of the sky.

The clouds are as disordered
as Harry Potter's hair
when he gets out of bed.

The sky is so immense
that even a gladiator can't hold it up.

The sky is a dreamworld
for birds that enjoy soaring to faraway lands.

**Lucy Auger (9)**
St Martin's School, Bournemouth

# Shark At Midnight

Shadows in the murky water
A shiver down my spine
A drop of blood could end my life
Always looking left and right
Thousands of teeth in every row
Don't know where to go
I toss and turn
My heart beats fast
A scream in the distance, or was it from my mouth?
Do I scream or do I shout?
Light in the distance
A feeling of warmth
A brush of something on my fingers
Suddenly I feel something solid beneath me
It's my bed
It was all just a dream
Although sharks can be quite scary in the dark.

**Connie Watts (9)**
St Martin's School, Bournemouth

# On Board

In my dreams, I can see the shimmering blue sea,
Splashing big waves at my old, creaky pirate ship and me.

The beautiful stars are like gold, glittery beacons
Leading my way to a lovely treasure island with golden chains and silver sequins.
In a tiny chest, in a small narrow hole,
You'll only find jewellery and no trace of coal.

Through the mist I can see
A tiny, rocky island coming closer and closer to me,
Whilst I'm listening to the lovely colourful tweeting birds humming their songs.

**Freddie Mussell (9)**
St Martin's School, Bournemouth

# Under The Sea

In my dreams every night,
Mermaids swim around the coral reef.
Sharks appear with big red eyes,
Scaring me with their big sharp teeth.

The mermaids ride dolphins every day,
And turtles are many, swimming around the bay.
There is a city under the sea,
Many people talk about it, but in my dreams I see.

I call it Atlantis City,
Which is so pretty.
Poseidon, the monster, wants me dead!
A swoosh of his trident made me sit up in my bed.

**Maya Benstead-Brooks-Dravecz (9)**
St Martin's School, Bournemouth

# I Dreamed That I Was In Space

**L** ying there I dreamt of a dream,
**O** ut in the dark, or so it seems,
**S** ky as dark as black octopus ink,
**T** oo much time to float and think.

**I** n a sea of shiny specks,
**N** ow all seems lost, what the heck?

**S** omehow, there's no oxygen left!
**P** sst goes the oxygen on my safety check,
**A** rgh!
**C** ome quick or I'm a goner,
**E** yes wide open!

**Rufus Stevens (9)**
St Martin's School, Bournemouth

# TV Dreams

A dream is just a TV show,
A special one for each night.
Tonight I dream of a waddle of penguins,
Who cuddle and hold each other tight.
The wind is freezing cold.
The ice beneath their feet,
It's hard like bulletproof glass,
Impossible to defeat.
They dive into the water to catch their prey
A delightful, silvery treat,
Their bellies are full like a summer's beach
And cover their tiny feet.

**Alex Broit (9)**
St Martin's School, Bournemouth

# Clowns

Clowns are scary, their lipstick's red,
People think they hide under your bed.
They try to be funny, but really they're not,
They just laugh, bounce, and dance a lot.
They are persuading you to laugh, ha ha ha,
They make the audience laugh by telling jokes and being a classic star.
They think they're funny, but they're actually loud,
Their skin is so pale, as pale a cloud.

**Rory Dennis (9)**
St Martin's School, Bournemouth

# Dragon Dream

The dragon creeps just like a snake, its nails scraping like a rake.
The wizard gets ready to shoot but the dragon slips down a laundry chute.
But that's when Sparkles comes in, she's hiding in a wheelie bin.
She creeps away so quietly and slick that the dragon falls for their trick.
The wizard comes down the chute but this time he's ready to shoot.

**Teddy Barker-Stock (9)**
St Martin's School, Bournemouth

# Monsters

**M** ale or female? Nobody knows,
**O** range scales and pointy toes,
**N** ails as thick as human bones,
**S** uspicious voice in a low sort of tone,
**T** eeth so sharp with a weird kind of smile,
**E** ager to have some food for a while,
**R** aging eyes as hard as stone,
**S** tumbling towards your home!

**Finn Dennis (9)**
St Martin's School, Bournemouth

# Dream Beans

I woke up to see a bean,
I hope I'm not too mean to the bean.

I take the bean and plant it,
I smell some fruity parsnips.

It came from next door,
They gave me some, I said, "Can I have some more?"

I go back home and eat some beans,
I was not too mean for the bean.

**Rupert Spencer (9)**
St Martin's School, Bournemouth

# When I Close My Eyes

As the lights turn off, I close my eyes.
The shimmering moon peers through my window,
I dream about the white, fluffy clouds,
Mushrooms and fantasy all around me.
I float myself to a woodland area,
I feel the bumpy texture of the wood
Leaves from the trees fall onto my head.

Now I become a teacher and then turn into an astronaut, walking on the moon!
I give myself wings,
I see the sun shining through crystals,
I glide into a dinosaur world,
My nose smells minty plants.

Now I'm a wizard with spells, wands and potions,
And I'm floating on a cloud,
As fairies rush past me,
Animals are down below.

I tap dance with my dance shoes back to my bed,
As the sun peers through my curtains once again with a bright glimmer,
I wait until the next night to dream it all again.

**Alice Walker (7)**
Winwick CE Primary School, Winwick

# Once Upon A Dream

**O** nce upon a dream,
**N** ight-time creeps upon the town,
**C** hildren sleeping like logs,
**E** veryone snoring, in a slumber.

**U** nder the duvet, people warm as ovens,
**P** ets all curled up in baskets,
**O** nly the night owl hoots,
**N** ight stars twinkle like golden jewels.

**A** ll the roads as quiet as mice.

**D** reams colour pictures in our minds,
**R** abbits down burrows, away from foxes,
**E** verything still as a statue,
**A** lyssa stirring from her sleep,
**M** orning comes to break the night.

**Alyssa Riley (7)**
Winwick CE Primary School, Winwick

# In A Dreamland

In a Dreamland so bright and fair,
My imagination took me there!

A unicorn with a bright pink tail,
Took me on a flight that never fails.

A rainbow river so bright and grand,
Makes me want to swim all through the land.

The flowers come alive with voices so sweet.
They giggle and chat and dance their feet.

The butterflies take flight in a dance of joy
And golden sunlight.
The roses whisper tales of life and delight.

So come to the garden where dreams come true,
In this enchanted world for evermore.

**Sophia Reeves (7)**
Winwick CE Primary School, Winwick

# Imagination

**I** magine a world full of dreams
**M** e and my friends playing like one team
**A** meal would be anything you like
**G** uessing games, it's a mindful delight
**I** n my world, we all unite
**N** ever stop believing in equal rights
**A** s we walk, we hear the rhythm of life
**T** o a different world, I travel every night
**I** t's a world full of everything you like
**O** h I hope all the colours of human life
**N** ever break apart or we will be lost without the colours of life.

**Asianne Chaudhry (8)**
Winwick CE Primary School, Winwick

# Once Upon A Football Dream

Once upon a football dream,
I played for a Premier League team,
Sometimes I played in the net,
I was the best that you could get.
When I played on the wing,
The speed of lightning I would bring,
When I kicked the ball,
I always gave my all.
When the ball hit the back of the net,
It was the best feeling you could get,
You could hear the crowd screaming,
Like it was in a dream.
I was the greatest of all time,
I heard the crowd begin to rhyme,
But now I must wake up,
To play in the FA Cup.

**George Lever (7)**
Winwick CE Primary School, Winwick

# The Story Behind My Eyes

It is Christmas in Wales,
Wind, rain and hailstones crashing
Against the windowpanes
No chimney for Santa, we need a magic key,
Sadness in my heart, missing my Christmas tree.
Mummy, Daddy, Nanny and Grandad are with me,
That makes me happy.
Don't worry as Santa knows we have a new magic key.
Santa and Rudolph will know where to find me,
Even though I'm not at home.
I'll still wake up on Christmas morning to my gifts,
And I won't be home alone.

**Esme Tilley-Stoneman (7)**
Winwick CE Primary School, Winwick

# Once Upon A Dream

I was going to the park
It was a gloomy evening
I was walking in the dark
I suddenly saw something with a spark
Then, I saw a million stars twinkling in the sky
With lots of chocolate bars
They saw me and called me twice
All of them were very nice
There, I had chocolate and ice cream
I wanted to eat more and more
But it was once upon a dream
Lots and lots of shining stars
And lots of ice cream
Oh, it was once upon a dream.

**Arjun Kankonkar (7)**
Winwick CE Primary School, Winwick

# Untitled

A place where superheroes fly,
Dragons soar up super, super high.
A place where forests are dark and vast,
My dog zooms by so brilliantly fast.
A place I can feel bright like the sun,
Yet the monsters come in and spoil the fun.
A place where the story can be good or bad,
But the morning comes, and I'm always glad.
I crawl into my mum's bed and share the theme,
Today is a new day, and it was just a dream.

**Charlie Cookson (7)**
Winwick CE Primary School, Winwick

# Dancing In The Jungle

A wet, stormy night, wrapped up nice and tight,
Dreams fill my head, lying comfy in bed.
We haven't stopped walking, we're too busy talking,
Deep in the jungle, what was that rumble?
It was the sound of the beat, we're moving our feet!
We're happy and free, my friends and me...
The lions, the snakes and a chimpanzee,
Dancing in the jungle, this is my dream.

**Ella Anders (7)**
Winwick CE Primary School, Winwick

# Football, Football, Football

**F** orever in her dreams to be in a team
**O** h how it makes her beam
**O** live on the pitch, there's never a hitch, sometimes may get a stitch
**T** ackle, pass, shoot, score
**B** ack of the net, what a roar!
**A** nother win
**L** ine up, shake hands, selfies with the fans
**L** ionel Messi better watch out.

**Olive Morris (7)**
Winwick CE Primary School, Winwick

# Playing Football

**F** ast football flying around the field.
**O** ver the net it goes!
**O** ooh! Close one.
**T** he football screams into the back of the net.
**B** *oom!*
**A** ll the fans roar.
**L** ucky goal!
**L** et's celebrate!

**Jake Thomas (7)**
Winwick CE Primary School, Winwick

# I Fly

Flying high in the sky,
Clouds passing by.
Flying faster than the speed of sound,
Night sky all around.
I see my house, it's time to land,
I can hardly stand!
So I lie down my head,
In my warm and cosy bed.

**James Bower (7)**
Winwick CE Primary School, Winwick

# A Surprise

A dark gloomy castle,
Towers as high as mountains,
In the corner, a friend appeared,
With green scales and skin like a dinosaur,
To my surprise,
He was mild,
He picked me up and took me home.

**Isaac Cotterill (7)**
Winwick CE Primary School, Winwick

# Football

I go to football with my dad.
I really want my team to win.
But if they play really bad.
I'm going to put my kit in the bin.

**Jack Holligan (8)**
Winwick CE Primary School, Winwick

# YOUNG WRITERS INFORMATION

We hope you have enjoyed reading this book – and that you will continue to in the coming years.

If you're a young writer who enjoys reading and creative writing, or the parent of an enthusiastic poet or story writer, do visit our website www.youngwriters.co.uk. Here you will find free competitions, workshops and games, as well as recommended reads, a poetry glossary and our blog.

If you would like to order further copies of this book, or any of our other titles, then please give us a call or visit www.youngwriters.co.uk.

Young Writers
Remus House
Coltsfoot Drive
Peterborough
PE2 9BF
(01733) 890066
info@youngwriters.co.uk

YoungWritersUK  YoungWritersCW
youngwriterscw  youngwriterscw